Can I Get a Little Help?

Can I Get a Little Help?

I'm Married! / I'm Single

J.K. HAMILTON

Can I Get a Little Help? I'm Married! / I'm Single
by J.K. Hamilton

Cover Design by Atinad Designs.

© Copyright 2015

SAINT PAUL PRESS, DALLAS, TEXAS

First Printing, 2015

All scripture quotations, unless otherwise listed, are taken from the Thompson Chain Reference Study Bible (King James Version).

ISBN-10: 0-9963241-5-1
ISBN-13: 978-0-9963241-5-1

Printed in the U.S.A.

Contents

Chapter 1: God's View of Marriage 9

Chapter 2: Ideas About Marriage 13

Chapter 3: Why Marriages Need Help 19

Chapter 4: Churches or Crutches? 23

Chapter 5: Unrealistic and Unmet "Sexpectations" 27

Chapter 6: God or Your Spouse:
Who Should You Please? 35

Chapter 7: The Original Design 43

Chapter 8: Being Together in Marriage 49

Chapter 9: Communication 55

Chapter 10: Restoring Communication 63

Chapter 11: The Challenge of Marriage.......................... 71

Chapter 12: What's Wrong with Being Single? 79

Chapter 13: Desperation: Compromises
and Complications 85

Chapter 14: A Strong Woman or the Wrong Woman? ... 91

Chapter 15: Examining Men 99

Chapter 16: Getting Married vs. Being Married 107

PART 1

Lord, I Need a Little Help Here, Please... I'm Married!

Chapter 1

God's View of Marriage

There are many views about marriage that are heavily influenced by the personal experiences of people. These various experiences account for the wide range of views on marriage. There are some who speak so well of marriage, based on their own positive experiences, that it almost nauseates those who have had negative marital experiences. On the other hand, there are others who speak so negatively about marriage that it strikes fear into the heart of anyone who is considering jumping the broom. However, it is important for children of God to align their view with God's view, despite their experiences. In other words, if God says a thing is "not good," then no matter how "good" it seems in human experience, it should still be defined by what God says rather than what our experience tells us. This principle applies just as much in the other direction. If God says a thing is "good," then no matter what a Christian's personal experience is with that thing, at the end of the day he must agree with God that it is good.

So it is with marriage. Read what God says about marriage:

- "And God said, it is not good that the man should be alone" (Gen. 2:18).
- "Marriage is honorable in all" (Heb. 13:4).

These Scriptures support God's perception of marriage as good and worthy of respect.

Now that we've established that marriage is good according to God, let's deal with why something that God says is good and respectable and honorable is not always good, respectable, and honorable in our human experience. We often experience conflict between God's IDEAL and our ORDEAL. This is not to suggest that every marriage is an ordeal, but I am suggesting that "good" doesn't come easy.

Since the beginning of time, anything and everything that God has made perfect has been tarnished by the enemy and the way of the world. I understand that some of you reading this book right now are in a great season of marriage, while others of you don't see your marriage lasting beyond this time next year. Whatever the case, some are left with the question: Can marriage really be good?

In considering your spouse, you may be thinking that he doesn't seem to respect you. He doesn't act like he desires you. She spends all of the money. She talks to you like a little child. He closes up and won't communicate. She's still attached to her daddy. You're competing with his momma. She won't stop being flirty. He still communicates with his exes. She talks *at* you and not *to* you. He's jealous and possessive. She challenges your leadership in front of people. He wants sex but doesn't know how to be romantic. She wants romance but makes excuses for not offering sex. He's angry at you all the time for no reason. She makes you pay for all her past hurts from previous relationships. He was unfaithful. She was unfaithful. He's not trying hard enough to look for a job. She won't cook. He's always on his phone texting God knows who. She talks about you to her friends.

The list of issues in marriage is infinite. I'm sure you're in at least two of these situations now. Yet, God sees this and still says, marriage is good? It almost doesn't make any sense.

No one would argue that having a car is anything but good. Yet in all honesty, although having a car is good, there are a myriad of malfunctions that can and will take place with a vehicle. The engine light comes on; there is a gas leak or an oil leak; the tires are balding; the computer system malfunctions; the catalytic converter, carburetor, or air stop working; there is wear and tear on the windshield wipers. The list can go on and on. However, just as maintenance is the key to keeping a good car good, maintenance is also key to keeping a good marriage good. Just because things malfunction at times with your vehicle it doesn't mean that vehicles are bad. And just because there are many potential dysfunctions in marriage it doesn't mean that marriage is bad.

It is important to understand that there is no marriage that exists successfully that the Lord has not aided in its success. In this book, I will address the various ways that the Lord helps our relationships that we sometimes don't recognize. There are obvious ways that troubled marriages are helped (counseling, advice, intervention), and there are some not-so-obvious ways that the Lord helps marriages (situational, circumstantial, designed devastation). In any case, successful marriages are not natural and don't just happen. Marriages need a little help from Heaven. Every now and then in my tenure as a married person, my marriage has even caused me to cry out to God and say, "Lord, a little help here, please. I'm married."

Chapter 2

Ideas About Marriage

More people are fascinated with the *idea* of marriage than with marriage itself. The idea of marriage is universal, but each marriage relationship is customized. Having counseled many couples during my tenure as a minister, it became apparent a long time ago that many partners hold each other accountable for not fulfilling their dreams of marriage, or even hold each other accountable for not being a replica of some other marriage relationship that appears to be perfect. This increases the pressure and unnecessary strain on any marriage. It's difficult to compete with an ideal. This principle does not only apply to the marriage relationship but to any relationship. There are several things that contribute to our ideas of marriage:

- Our family of origin
- Movies
- Advice, both good and bad
- Talk shows and talk show hosts
- Literature: religious and nonreligious
- Other marital relationships

This list creates expectations for many who will get or have gotten married. Are these expectations fair? Are they realistic? Are they possible? To these questions, this is my answer: Some of these expectations are fair, but many are not. Some of these expectations are realistic and others are fictitious. Some of these expectations are possible, but many of them are not probable. Again, while the fundamental principles of marriage apply to all (fidelity, communication, trust), every marriage has its own DNA. By DNA I mean DIRECTION, NATURE, and APPROACH.

There are different roads to marital success. These roads are customized in each marriage based on the experiences the couple has had together and as individuals. This determines each marriage's DIRECTION. Every marriage also has its own nature, meaning how each couple's vibe is different from other couples' vibe. The NATURE of a marriage often has to do with values, principles, standards, desires, personalities, and personal characteristics. The APPROACH of a marriage has to do with how each individual manages change, conflict, decision-making, crisis, pain, and joy.

Now, I know this sounds like a lot of marital psychology and much of it is psychological. However, because I've been called to be a man of faith, I contend that God even influences psychology within the institution of marriage. I believe the influence that couples allow God to have over these psychological aspects of marriage determines whether their marital outcome is successful. In simpler terms, when a couple's DIRECTION, NATURE, and APPROACH (DNA) are influenced by the will of God, then there is nothing that can't be worked out and overcome in marriage. However, it absolutely, positively is a two-person endeavor. Husband and wife should be like-minded concerning the will of God.

I know what some of you may be asking: "What if I got married young and was not really ready?" To this I answer, if God was able to keep marriages together that were arranged by other people (i.e., Isaac and Rebekah, Moses and Zipporah {somewhat}, and others), then He's able to keep marriages together that were not given much forethought. However, I do not suggest that marriage should be jumped into spontaneously and without much thought and preparation. What I am saying is this: If God can raise the dead, then He definitely can heal sick things, even if those sick things are marriages.

So how does God help a marriage? I'm not so naive as to believe that the only eyes reading this book are the eyes of people in ideal situations. The very title of the book was enough to generate interest in delving a little deeper to find solutions to questions you've contemplated in your lonely quiet moments concerning your marriage.

Well, in the rest of Part 1 of this book, we will look at a few ways that the Lord helps and influences the DIRECTION, NATURE, AND APPROACH of our marriage relationships. I've seen the Lord do it in my own marriage. As a matter of fact, He's not finished putting the varnish on my marriage. My marriage is constantly evolving because my wife and I are constantly evolving individually. Yet, the question still remains: How does Heaven help marriages?

In His earthly ministry, our Lord always had a tendency to address the root before He addressed the fruit. In Luke 13: 6–9, the dresser of the vineyard asked the master to give him time to fertilize and dig about the root so that it might produce fruit. You see, even in marriages, a fruit problem may be a root problem. In John 4, the woman at the well has a problem keeping her marriage, so Jesus goes deeper to the root of the problem, which of course turns out to be her attempt to satisfy her thirst in life by artificial nonsustaining means. Our Lord wastes no time or energy making the fruit look good if the root is not good. There are a lot of polished marriages with dead roots. In the next few chapters, we will explore some root issues and fruit issues, and suggest ways that the Lord will cultivate a marriage so it not only survives but also thrives.

Chapter 3
Why Marriages Need Help

Before hastily and hurriedly getting into how God helps marriages, I want to explore why marriages need help in the first place.

Becoming One Takes Time

As soon as the vows are repeated before the judge or the preacher, the deal is sealed with a kiss and the marriage license is signed. A man and his wife will go on with one name. In my case, Jamell K. Hamilton and Carole M. Burnett became Mr. and Mrs. Hamilton. Just like that, in an instant, two people became one in NAME and in the THEORY of matrimony. Though becoming one in name is instant, becoming one in DNA (direction, nature, and approach) is a process. It's a process that can be vigorous and tempestuous and even downright uncomfortable at times. The process of becoming one will often involve disagreements, arguments, misunderstandings, and moments of frustration, disappointment, offensive words, and a host of other things that will make you wonder if it's even worth it. As a matter of fact, there are many people who give up on their marriages in the middle of the process of becoming one with their spouses. Time, tolerance, and patience are the ingredients for enduring the process. There are some things that matter in the beginning of the marriage relationship that become less important with time and process. There are certain arguments that eventually become null and void with time and process. Just as time and process facilitate physical growth to the point where there are some shoes that you wore in your lifetime that you will never fit again, time and process facilitate marital growth to the point where there are some issues that will never be priorities again in your marriage. They will no longer fit where you are in your marriage relationship.

"Self": The Destroyer

Post-sin (after sin entered the world), humanity became selfish and self-centered. Selfishness is and has been at the core of sin since its origin in the

Garden of Eden. God created us without the germ of selfishness. There was no sense of self-awareness. This was so much the case that Adam and Eve had no awareness of their nakedness: "And they were both naked, the man and his wife and were not ashamed" (Gen. 2:25). They had a strong God consciousness and had a strong awareness of each other. Adam never bragged about his own body or existence, but when he saw Eve it almost seemed as if he was fascinated with this being with a body compatible to his. Genesis 2:23 states this: "This is now bone of my bone and flesh of my flesh... she shall be called woman." It wasn't until sin entered the world that they both began looking at themselves and noticing their own nakedness, and in their shame desperately attempted to cover themselves. In Genesis 3:7, we see the birth of self-awareness, which in the extreme results in selfishness and self-centeredness. It says, "And the eyes of them both were opened, and they knew that they were naked."

Since the introduction of self-awareness, it has been at the core of just about every trespass, abomination, transgression, sin, and offense committed in relationships, including the marital relationship. Because this can be the case in marriages, it must mean that one of the greatest impediments to a couple becoming one in DNA is selfishness: What I want. What I need from you. How it makes *me* feel. You need to listen to *me*. *I* want you to do this, that, or the other. You don't make *me* feel like a woman/man. Marriage relationships today are often not entered into to give but to receive. This is the way of selfishness. Self has a good history of draining marriages of the joy of union and turning the dream of a happy union into the nightmare of unhappy bondage. Self is a destroyer that finds its way into every aspect of your marriage relationship and spreads like a malignant growth until it forces the marriage into a comatose state. Self will infiltrate your finances. Despite having plans of building capital, Self says, "Because I make the money I can spend it like I want to." Selfishness will infiltrate sexuality: "If I don't get it here, I'll get it somewhere else" or "You need to do this or that for me." Selfishness will use sex for the climax and not for the bond it can create.

Selfishness will infiltrate communication and monopolize it, leaving one spouse to speak while the other always has to just listen. Selfishness will infiltrate every aspect of a marriage; it is a destroyer. However, the Lord has a way of helping a marriage built on selfishness by wearing down Self. This is not always a comfortable process.

Chapter 4

Churches or Crutches?

There are many issues in marriage that go unaddressed, particularly in the sometimes sterile environment of the church. For some strange reason, the setting that God designed for us to present ourselves as we are often turns out to be the environment where we present ourselves as we want to be viewed and perceived. It's a mentality deeply embedded in the idea of "presenting God with your best," as I always heard in the church when I was coming up as a child. The problem with that idea is that it often causes us to leave our best at the altar on Sunday and then walk out of the sanctuary into the next week with only that which causes us to fall short of the Lord's glory. This causes the church to become a breeding ground of secrecy, hidden hurt, hidden pain, and unresolved issues.

This idealistic imagery is even more problematic in our marriages. There are many couples who have mastered adorning themselves in the garb of marital bliss only to get home from church, disrobe, and find themselves in the naked truth of their marital discontent and misery. "But we can't let the church folks see us like this," they say to themselves. This is often the reason there is such a high level of shock and disbelief when a marriage dissolves; it seems to be out of the blue. The reality is that it's never out of the blue. Marital decay is gradual, no matter how well the exterior of a marriage is maintained. Sometimes the church is used as the very crutch that enables a marriage to hobble along in its weakened state. Think about it. The church is often an environment where people know you on a surface level, and they commend what they see on Sundays. People often make conclusions about your marital relationship based on a once-a-week fleeting observation.

There are many couples who are commendable in the public eye while being incorrigible in the eyes of God. Couples, then, may become more comfortable in the environment where they are seen the way they want to be seen as opposed to being seen the way they are. And what environment is that? You guessed it: the church, the place where rotting marriage relationships can appear polished and pristine. Statistically, people's coworkers are more inclined to hear about their marital distress than their church families. Thus, the church becomes the crutch that people lean on to develop their belief in their own upstanding marriage. However, the great news is that God's vision is not limited to what we show Him on Sundays. No matter how well Carole and I are seen as a couple by the congregants of the church where we minister, God does not deal with us according to popular opinion, but according to His knowledge of us. This is a blessing, because there is often no help for people who are perceived by others as always having it together. At the end of the day, we face the same realities and challenges that are faced by other couples.

The only way to get help from Heaven for your marriage is to stop looking at your marriage the way it SHOULD be and look at it the way it IS. Trust God to close the gap between your marital "should be" and your marital "is." Be true to yourselves as a couple, and don't become intoxicated by the well-meaning perceptions of others. See your marriage the way God sees it, and speak of it as God would speak of it, so that the church will not become the place where you master the art of camouflaging your marriage with bliss and become "crutched" by the church. The Lord is not in the business of simply relieving but healing, and without a revealing there is no healing. This is the principle behind getting blood work done at a doctor's visit. If it were enough to say, "I feel better," then you may leave the visit both ignorant and sick. Thus, blood is drawn and through the blood test comes a revealing of what's going on so that the doctor does not prescribe medicine based on how you feel, but based on what the test reveals. God longs to heal your marriage. But who would declare that their marriage relationship was healed in an environment that says you're okay? Or what couple would be inclined to give glory to God for a healed marriage if they never acknowledged that their marriage was sick? The church is the body of Christ (Col. 1:18), and Christ cares about what ails His body, even if it's your marriage. Deliverance... not just relief; change... not just crutches.

Chapter 5

Unrealistic and Unmet "Sexpectations"

A nother issue that couples have a tendency to avoid or bury their heads in the sand about is sexuality in marriage. Notice I stated "sex in marriage." Outside of marriage it's called fornication, despite how socially acceptable it might be. Sometimes couples need Heaven's help in this area. In spite of how practical this subject is, many couples choose not to pray about their marital sexuality. However, there is not a crevice of our lives that we don't need the Lord in. We even need the Lord in the bedroom.

Where do sexual expectations come from in marriage? How do they develop? How are they enforced? One look at the "first couple" will teach us volumes about sexual expectations. It appears that first man, Adam, had more of a fascination with Eve coming OUT of him than with him going INTO Eve. Look at the text:

Then the Lord God made a woman from the rib, and he brought her to the man.

> "At last!" the man exclaimed.
> "This one is bone from my bone,
> and flesh from my flesh
> because she was taken from 'man.'"
> (Gen. 2: 22–26)

There doesn't appear to be a lot of preoccupation with sex, even though I'm sure they enjoyed it and engaged in it regularly. Neither does there appear to be any evidence of expectation. Why? Because expectation derives from experience. Perhaps because Adam had no prior sexual experience he had no expectations when it came to sex with his wife. It must have been sheer fireworks! For Adam to have absolutely nothing to compare his experience with Eve to and vice versa must have made for excellent sex. Unfortunately, in the world we live in today, there are very few people who go into the marriage bed without expectations. On the contrary, for many people, by the time they get to the marriage bed, they've had so many experiences that they carry these experiences into the honeymoon suite and expect from their bride or groom a performance equal to experiences in their past. This is unfair and unrealistic, and often ultimately fatal to a marriage.

There is a plethora of experiences people go through that influence their sexual expectations. When I was a pre-teen I was exposed to pornography. Looking back, I realize that this was my first sexual experience, and even though it was virtual, it was an experience nonetheless. This experience gave birth to expectations in my mind of what should happen during sex—expectations of how my wife should respond to what I do to her, even the faces that should be made in the process. As soon as I had this premature experience it robbed my wife (whoever she would be—years later) of being accepted as she is, and it made her a competitive lover. The expectations that come as a result of experiences that we should have never encountered are unrealistic and unfair. This applies to every premature sexual encounter. They cause a marriage to begin under the pressure of comparison. If wives and husbands are not careful they will find themselves looking to duplicate a past experience in their present marriage. It can then turn into an insatiable appetite for the original high of a pleasurable past experience. Such experiences heighten expectations, which can then trigger experimentation; this is unrealistic, unfair, impure, and uncouth. This is not just something husbands do, but wives as well. An honest heart will admit that this is a real challenge in marriage and can only be helped by Heaven. This explains why it is so potentially destructive to use pornography. If you watch Jezebel in action long enough, you'll forget that you're married to Martha when in the bedroom. If you watch Mandingo long enough, you'll forget that you're married to Henry when in the bedroom. I think you get the picture.

So how is this remedied if you've had a series of premature sexual encounters? First of all, your sex life in your marriage is worth praying about. So start. God wants to fill every part of your being and your life. His power gives us everything we need for life and Godliness (2 Pet. 1:3). So just as you pray about your job, your health, your family, and your children, pray about your bedroom activities with your spouse. Ask God to save you from the temptation and practice of adultery (mental or physical) by either neutralizing your drive or increasing your spouse's. I know this is easier said than done, but your marriage depends on it. Second, refocus on what enamored Adam about Eve: that she came out of him and that she belonged to him. There is a certain amount of sexual desire that's generated when I see my wife in the splendor of her beauty and think, "That's mine right there," or "She was made for me." You see, what you think in your HEAD determines the kind of experience you will have in your BED.

Also, always remember that a great sandwich has more than bread and meat. What do you mean? you may ask. There are things you can add to a sandwich that will intensify its taste. Lettuce, tomatoes, onion, mayo, honey mustard, olives, etc. If you only use meat and bread, don't complain that your sandwich always tastes the same. God has given you the right to be as creative as you want to be within the boundaries of mutual consent and Godly standards. By mutual consent, I mean the agreement of both spouses (otherwise it becomes an act of selfish gratification or even sexual violation). By Godly standards, I mean within the way God set up marriage: one husband, one wife, belonging solely to each other in one union. Creativity becomes sinful when it violates the basic principles of marriage.

The other side of this coin is, one of the quickest ways to set your marriage up for failure due to sexual frustration is unnecessary deprivation. Listen to the apostle Paul in 1 Corinthians 7: 3–5:

> The husband should fulfill his wife's sexual needs, and the wife should fulfill her husband's needs.
>
> The wife gives authority over her body to her husband, and the husband gives authority over his body to his wife.

Do not deprive each other of sexual relations.

Sometimes you may both agree to refrain from sexual intimacy for a limited time so you can give yourselves more completely to prayer. Afterward, you should come together again so that Satan won't be able to tempt you because of your lack of self-control.

These Scriptures show that sexuality clearly comes with the package of marriage. What person would want to work on a job for years with absolutely no benefits? One of the most frustrating things for me is when I order food from a drive-thru, perhaps a combo that should include fries and a drink. I pay for the combo and drive off only to get down the road and discover that they left out the fries. If I've gone too far I just settle for a meal without them, but it does not erase the fact that at the window I paid for them. Well, the marriage altar is a lot like that drive-thru window. You make agreements and vows and it is a travesty to get down the road only to discover that the "French fries of frolic" are not in the bag, or that someone forgot to put your "passion pepper" in the bag, or the "booty bacon" (I think you get the point).

The principle outlined in the aforementioned verse is unisex. It applies to both the husband and the wife who have sex as a right and privilege part of the commitment of marriage. Now, I am not suggesting that both spouses must have the same appetite, but they should at least both dine at the same table. Unmet needs can lead to a Satanic set-up. The enemy knows how to appeal to your deprivation and generate desperation. And desperate people have a tendency to settle. I used to often wonder why a man can be married to an intelligent, well kept, classy, spiritual, educated, and extremely beautiful woman, only to turn around and fall in with someone who doesn't possess half of those qualities. Could it be it's because a hamburger that you can eat is better than a lamb chop on display? I think you get the point.

The apostle Paul urged his readers in the church at Corinth not to play games with the fire of passion. I do understand why this would be an issue, considering that Corinth was notorious for its temple of Aphrodite where one thousand prostitutes were available and willing to satisfy any patron. Paul was saying to both husbands and wives, "Don't create an environment at home that makes the environment in the temple attractive." I believe that if Paul were here today, he would echo his previous words, especially considering the times we live in.

When you set your husband or wife up for failure to maintain sexual integrity due to intentional deprivation (not circumstantial, such as sickness, etc.), although he or she will be judged guilty by God for biting the worm off of another hook, you will also be accountable for not putting anything on your hook to bite. I'm just saying.

Chapter 6

God or Your Spouse: Who Should You Please?

Someone once said, "The only person I need to please is God!" This statement, as bold, bad, and confident as it sounds is only a half-truth at best. Yes, God is the primary person we should all seek to please; however, pleasing God also includes being pleasing to your spouse. This is by God's design. If you don't want to have to be pleasing to people, then it's best that you remain unmarried. Deciding to get married involves agreeing to please a husband or wife. You can't harvest all of the benefits of marriage and discard all of the responsibilities. This is the way of the world: to always want something for nothing, more for less, a title without responsibility, a marriage without a commitment. However, it is not so with God. Listen to what the apostle Paul told the church in Corinth:

I want you to be free from the concerns of this life. An unmarried man can spend his time doing the Lord's work and thinking how to please him.

But a married man has to think about his earthly responsibilities and how to please his wife.

His interests are divided. In the same way, a woman who is no longer married or has never been married can be devoted to the Lord and holy in body and in spirit. But a married woman has to think about her earthly responsibilities and how to please her husband. (1 Cor. 7: 32–35; NLT)

So, you see, when you decided to get married, by default you took on the responsibility of pleasing your spouse. However, what happens when your efforts to please your spouse are met with resistance, ungratefulness, expectation, or lack of reciprocity? Are you released of your marital responsibility to please your spouse if they make no efforts to please you? Is reciprocity a condition of your responsibility? What happens when you begin to feel like you're doing all of the pleasing? These are real questions and real challenges that married couples face both in and out of the body of Christ. And if these issues are not addressed, marriages will go from blessed to blasted, blissful to blistered, romantic to frantic, from "little house on the prairie" to a "nightmare on Elm Street." So while you may not care much whether or not you're doing a good job pleasing people at your job or at church or amongst your kinfolk, marriage requires you to be concerned with pleasing your spouse.

There are very few marital frustrations that rival the frustration of attempting to please someone who refuses to be pleased. Pleasing your spouse can at times be one of the most draining, tedious, and worrisome tasks. And then at other times it can be the most fulfilling, satisfying, and joyful part of marriage. It really all depends on the attitude and disposition of both parties. Some of you reading this book can attest to the fact that sometimes it seems as if nothing is enough. If you cook for him it wasn't the meal he wanted. If you buy her flowers she would rather you had taken her out. If you clean the house until it's spotless you should have taken his clothes to the cleaners. If you give her money to get her nails done she would rather you had taken her to the salon yourself. He doesn't like how you talk to him. She wants you to clean up and cook after you come home from work, even though she was home all day. He wants you to slave like superwoman all day at your job and then be wonder woman at night in the bedroom. You don't do this, that, or the other thing right. You should've done this instead of that. The list goes on and on. If you don't manage the frustration that comes with the challenge of pleasing your spouse it can literally drive you (husbands and wives) into a depressive state. Then, to add to the frustration of bending over backwards to please your spouse, you seldom get the sense that your efforts are appreciated.

This feeling of not being appreciated is often used by the devil to lead a spouse to do things for others just for the gratification of feeling appreciated. You start cooking for your coworker because he seems to like and appreciate your dishes. You start helping your coworker with some of her bills because she lets you know how much you've helped her. You'd rather be like a superhero who would save the day for someone who at least says, "Thank you! You're my hero," than be there to save your own wife. Your husband has grown so accustomed to you as superwoman that he no longer seems to see how "super" you really are. Gratitude is eclipsed by expectation.

I'm reminded of a story about a little boy whose grandma takes him with her to church. One Sunday an old brother from the church walks up to her grandson, stoops down, and gives him an orange.

His grandma smiles and says to her grandson, "That was so nice, grandson, now what do you say?" The little boy looks at the orange then looks at the old man who has given it to him and replies, "Peel it." The boy is so full of expectations that he can't take the time to show gratitude. He wants more before he says thank you for what has already been done for him. This is the same as it is with some marriages. Hubby or wife wants more even though he or she never takes the time to say thank you for what has already been done or what has already been given.

So, what is the answer? Is there help from Heaven on whether to please or not to please? Absolutely! First of all, realize that the only person who the Lord gave you the power to control is YOU. Not your wife. Not your husband. YOU! When it comes to everyone else God gave us the power to *influence*. And the best mechanism of influence is being an example. As a husband or wife, you should BE whatever you want to SEE. The apostle Peter drives this principle home, particularly to wives:

> In the same way, you wives must accept the authority of your husbands. Then, even if some refuse to obey the Good News, your godly lives will speak to them without any words. They will be won over by observing your pure and reverent lives. (1 Pet. 3:1–2; NLT)

Influence. Modeling. Being an example. The message in this passage was to wives, but the principle applies equally to husbands as well.

Second, pray that the Lord helps you to see that you are appreciated even when you seldom hear it. I know what you may be thinking: "I need to hear it every now and then." Your feelings are certainly legitimate, but hearing it while not seeing it might be a little worse. The proof is always in the behavior. Words are as invisible as the wind if not followed up by action. In addition, focus more on how God is pleased when you seek to please your spouse according to God's will. When your primary focus is on pleasing the Lord, if your spouse does not change, then the Lord will change you. He will reshape your desire and expectations so that you seek God's "well done" more than your spouse's "thank you."

On a more practical level, make some time to pamper, nurture, and minister to yourself. Embracing a healthy outlet is a good way to do this. Just as Jesus, Himself, took a break from ministering to the masses, as did His disciples, by going to a lonely place to pray, reboot, and release, so should you. Find a quiet place to exhale. Take a drive, go to the golf course, walk around a park, go sit by a pond, get your nails done, catch a matinee movie, go eat at a restaurant, sit in Starbucks and read, go to Walmart and sit on the bench and watch people walk by, or go to the gym. There are a myriad of outlets through which you can restore the energy it takes to please your spouse. This becomes intensely important especially in situations where you are trying to please someone who never seems to be satisfied. I've learned and seen that sometimes people can get so accustomed to *receiving* that, for fear of having to *give*, they act as if what they receive is never enough. There are husbands who do this to keep their wives in a position of always doing and giving. There are wives who do this because it's a very comfortable place for them, a place they don't want to leave. Whatever the case, God's design was for man to give as a husband and woman to give as a wife. I've learned that each person's part becomes easy to do when each person does his part. To please or not to please, that is the question—and the answer.

Chapter 7
The Original Design

It may not be a bad idea for married persons to familiarize themselves with how God originally designed the marriage relationship. Everything that God established was flawless. This even includes the marriage relationship. One look back to the beginning will reveal that God established marriage (through exclusivity), blessed marriage (through union and procreation), and then insulated marriage (through separation). This may sound like a lot of theological jargon, but it really is quite practical. Let's revisit these three aspects of God's original blueprint of marriage.

God established marriage through exclusivity. God certainly had the option when He sedated Adam and performed the first surgical procedure in history: He could have taken two ribs and made him two women to choose from. However, this was not God's design. That God only brought one woman to Adam was indicative of God's design for marriage as an exclusive relationship: one man, one woman, for life. Adam's attention was not divided between Eve and Evelyn. There was one marital focus. There was one marital bond. There was one marital relationship. Adam called Eve "bone of my bone and flesh of my flesh." How confusing this would have been if God had given Adam several choices. But He didn't. He didn't because God's design for marriage was an EXCLUSIVE relationship.

God blessed the marriage through their union and procreation. No matter our view of marriage today, we must be honest enough to acknowledge how God designed marriage. People shouldn't hate the original design because it's been tarnished and broken in their experience. We must uphold God's original purpose no matter how far we have fallen from it in our own lives. God blessed them to multiply themselves by the principle of "every seed after its kind." This means that in God's original blueprint, family was designed to reproduce family to reproduce family. Also, the gift of sexual union is not only for procreation but also for affirmation and recreation. This was all designed within the exclusive relationship of marriage. This is how He blessed their union. Marital union is not a passive union but a passionate union.

Finally, in God's original design, marriage was to be insulated from outside interference. The Bible declares that "for this cause should a man leave father and mother and cleave to his wife and the two shall become one flesh" (Gen. 2:24). This means that God's original design of the marriage relationship was a table for two and only two. Thus, the marriage relationship is insulated from outside influences.

This last aspect is where this chapter will hang its hat. Another threat to the marriage relationship is when there are too many people at this table for two. There is to be no greater influence here on earth than the influence of a husband or wife. The closed marriage relationship is a marriage that will never meet its demise because of outside forces and voices. When a husband or a wife invites family, friends, and others into their marriage by sharing personal information, it makes the marriage relationship vulnerable. Someone reading this book may be asking, "What if I just need someone to talk to?" This is a legitimate issue, and having a good dependable outlet is sometimes needful. However, be very selective with your outlets, otherwise you may find yourself walking in the counsel of the ungodly, or standing in the way of sinners, or sitting in the seat of the scornful (Psalm 1:1). A common mistake that husbands and wives make in moments of marital frustration is inviting certain unqualified people to take a look into their marital chaos and involving them into a situation that they aren't vested in. The problem with this is that once you unveil your marital frustrations to certain people you also make your spouse vulnerable to them. Pay attention to the following scenarios:

- A wife confides in her single girlfriend about how dissatisfied she is with her husband and makes light of how she starves him of sex, not realizing that by default she's displaying her husband's vulnerability to someone who may be privately imagining how much she would appreciate a man like that.

- A husband confides in "his boys" about how his wife doesn't satisfy him and how he thinks she is lazy and clueless, not realizing that one of his boys may not see the same thing and now wants to sympathize with her in the absence of her husband.

- A wife demeans her husband because of everything he doesn't do for her to a woman who doesn't have anyone and who has to do everything for herself—including things that a husband would do for her.

- A man talks to his partner about how much he wants out of his marriage, and his partner thinks how he wouldn't mind being a superman and savior to the man's wife, and how much better a job he could do for her.

- A wife talks to her parents about her marital frustrations. Her parents then begin to develop an ongoing disdain for the woman's husband that outlasts her moment of frustration.

- A husband is a "mama's boy" and invites his mother into his marital frustrations. This slowly deteriorates his mother's respect for his wife. Ultimately, this leads to his mother's inadvertent and almost unintentional attempts to pour salt on the marriage's open wound.

These are just some of the ways inviting OUTSIDERS into the marital relationship can hinder and interfere with the healing and restoration processes, and can intensify and expose the vulnerability of a spouse. You see, the reality is, frustration may be momentary, but the information shared will outlast the moment of frustration. When the problem subsides, you are left with this person who may still retain the frustration that you shared or perhaps may see your marriage relationship as fake or insincere.

Is there help from Heaven when seeking someone to talk with? Absolutely. Pray for discretion and wisdom. The Lord will give you sound advice. Consult a counselor, minister, therapist, or spiritually-minded friend who will not change his perceptions of you or your spouse after the frustrations are shared, discussed, and prayed about. God will lead you to someone who won't bring it up every time they see you and your spouse after you have reconciled. But most of all, seek God's wisdom. Talk to God just as personally as you would talk to a friend or family member. He hears and knows and sees. The Lord will bless your marriage through the mess of the moment. And long after it's resolved He won't look at you or your spouse differently. Keep two chairs at the table of your marriage. The only people who should be standing around your table are those who are waiting on you in prayer. The Lord set the table for TWO and TWO only; don't pull up any other chairs. Leave it the way God set it up.

Chapter 8

Being Together in Marriage

L ooking back over my own marriage, I admit that there has been a lot of time wasted over the years. As a matter of fact, many married people inadvertently waste a lot of time throughout their tenure in marriage. Time is a precious commodity that can't be bought with money, regained if lost, or slowed down or sped up, and everything about it is uncertain. When you think about it, we don't have as much time as we think we have. Though Carole and I have been together for several years, the reality is, we haven't spent all of those years together. Being together and spending time together are two different things. They are absolutely not synonymous. There are many couples who have been together for years but have only spent days together.

One critical look at how a day is divided will prove this theory. Generally, eight hours is spent working, eight hours is spent sleeping, which leaves eight hours to spend time together. Those eight hours that are left are often divided up between taking care of business, the affairs of children, chores, and other duties. Thus, the eight hours that are left may actually be reduced to about four hours: just four hours a day to spend time together, if that much. This means it would take six days to have spent twenty-four hours with your spouse. If every six days you spend a day's worth of time with each other, in a year you would spend approximately sixty days together. Now this doesn't include the days that your job has you out of town or doing overtime, or other personal circumstances taking up your time together. You see, that's really not a lot of time, and since that's not a lot of time, then it's important that the time that is spent together is of good quality. Look at what the Word says about the brevity of time:

- "See then that ye walk circumspectly, not as fools, but as wise, Redeeming the time, because the days are evil" (Eph. 5:15-16).

- "Whereas ye know not what *shall be* on the morrow. For what *is* your life? It is even a vapour, that appeareth for a little time, and then vanisheth away" (James 4: 14).

- "The days of our years *are* threescore years and ten; and if by reason of strength *they be* fourscore years, yet *is* their strength labour and sorrow; for it is soon cut off, and we fly away" (Psalm 90:10).
- "Man is like to vanity: His days *are* as a shadow that passeth away" (Psalm 144: 4).

So you see, time is already short. Then you subtract all the ways we have to spend our time to survive and time gets even shorter.

There are many things in a marriage that unnecessarily consume a great deal of time. Ain't nobody got time for these things (in the words of Sweet Brown). There are some situations that steal from the sixty plus days a year that you and your spouse have together. Here are a few things that are notorious for stealing time away from you and your spouse (and ain't nobody got time for these things):

The silent treatment. This is one of the most effective thieves of time and also one of the most common. Using silence in a passive-aggressive way to protest whatever situation upsets you minimizes the quality time that can be spent together building instead of battling. The silent treatment is when a spouse turns inward instead of openly discussing the matter or offence. This closes the spouse's spirit to his partner (with silence) in an effort to silently scold them for the offence. When asked, "What's wrong?" the reply is generally "nothing," so as to continue the torment of silence. The time that's spent being closed could be used discussing and resolving the matter so that you don't waste the four hours of quality time you have in a day. There are times when quieting your spirit is necessary to regulate your emotions, but it's important to BE over it when you GET over it… because ain't nobody got time for the silent treatment.

Sleeping apart. Many people can relate to this — myself included. Sometimes you just see your spouse as the enemy, and who wants to sleep with the enemy? There's a country and western song that I once heard while radio station surfing. The name or message of the song was "I don't want to kiss the lips at night that's been talking crap all day." This is often the sentiment many couples have at some point in their marriage history. Sometimes the tranquility that comes with sleeping alone feels much better than the chill of laying beside a spouse who seems to be cold-blooded. And yes, there are times that may even necessitate taking a little break. However, couples should swiftly attempt to resolve issues that cause this bedroom rift. Paul tells the church in Ephesus to be "angry and sin not: let not the sun go down on your wrath. Neither give place to the devil" (Eph. 4:26–27). This is also a thief of the little time you and your spouse actually have together. It's very difficult to think like this in the heat of the situations that come up, but at the end of the day each small situation must not be seen as the bigger picture. As excruciating as it may be to go into the bedroom and lay next to the person who got on your nerves you should bring yourself to do it. Who knows? An unintentional touch in the middle of the night might lead to joy in the morning. Sleeping apart, though? Ain't nobody got time for that.

Staying away from home for extended periods of time. Wise man Solomon declared in Proverbs 21:19: "It is better to dwell in the wilderness, than with a contentious and an angry woman." This Scripture lets us know that there are times when it is better to be away. The principle is applicable to both women and men. As a matter of fact, the same Solomon who talked about an angry women says in Proverbs 22:24: "Make no friendship with an angry man; And with a furious man thou shalt not go." So you see, there is great legitimacy in getting away. But also bear in mind that extended periods away from home because of frustration can be a breeding ground for temptation. If you need to "dwell in the wilderness" for a while, then by all means dwell in the wilderness. But when the fires of frustration cool down, it may be a good idea to hurry home lest the devil has his way with you in your vulnerable state. Ain't nobody got time for that.

There are a plethora of other examples that I could give, but I believe you can see the point. Time is precious and once it's wasted it cannot be recaptured. Some issues do not warrant the extremity to which we sometimes react to them. Four hours a day is not much, but it can be enough if the quality of that time is meaningful and purposeful. If it won't matter tomorrow, then it's worth getting over today because remember: ain't nobody got time for that.

Chapter 9
Communication

If I were to take a poll of married couples about what they believe is the single most important facet of marriage apart from God as the center, many of them would say communication. Communication is essential for marital success. Now, when I use the term "marital success," I'm not referring to a flawless, fail-proof, problem-safe, drama-free marriage. I actually believe that real love never comes without those challenges. However, I am referring to a marriage that lasts in spite of the drama, problems, failures, and flaws. Every now and then I hear some couple make declarations such as "We've never argued or fought in all the years we've been together." While I don't believe this is impossible, I have to wonder if they live together. Because it would be easy to always get along in two different cities; but under the same roof? Highly improbable. Communication is one of the issues that develops with time. How it develops is up to each couple. Communication can be a growing muscle in your marriage or a growing tumor in your marriage, depending on what kind of communication is prevalent in your relationship. In this chapter I want to talk about four types of communication in marriage: good communication, bad communication, NO communication, and ugly communication.

We learn communication long before we decide to marry someone. We're exposed to communication in childhood through the communication of our parents or caregivers. It's been said that we will either duplicate the kind of communication we were exposed to or we will completely avoid what we've been exposed to and go to the opposite extreme. For example, the man who grew up seeing his daddy cusses, disrespects, and abuses his mother will either do the same thing to his wife, or else he may become extremely passive toward her. Or the woman who grew up seeing her mother run down her daddy or other men verbally will either do it to her husband or else be very passive and accommodating. Now, it's not as extreme in every case, but these are just some examples of the influence of what we've been exposed to can have on our marriages. Many husbands and wives who are not necessarily in favor of being like their parents will often declare, "I'm not going to be like my dad/mom," while all along unknowingly demonstrating some of the very qualities of their parents. As you read this book, even if this is not your situation, I'm sure you know of couples for whom this is an issue. There is a host of other factors that play a part in why we communicate the way we do in our marriages, far too many to mention. There are some who actually hope for their spouse to communicate the way their father or mother communicated. When they do not, it can cause a rift in communication because of unmet expectations about communication. Again, I can go on and on with scenarios, but I want to talk about what good communication is.

There are certain ingredients that are necessary for *good communication* in a marriage. My cellular service is with AT&T and has been for years. It's because my experience with them has been very pleasing. This means that the messages are clear coming in and going out. It means that I have coverage even in unlikely places, and I have a large coverage area. It also means that I have very few dropped calls. These are the basic things that make my experience with AT&T very good. Ironically, these are the basic principles of good communication in marriage. Clear signals, good reception, good range, and few dropped calls.

When couples clearly and honestly express themselves and communicate their wants, likes, needs, feelings, ideas, and opinions to one another through active listening and conversation, then the signals are clear. It's amazing how many couples don't really know their spouse. It's very possible to be married for years and not really know your spouse because of a lack of communication. In marriages, especially new marriages, it is very important to be honest, open, vulnerable, and transparent in communication, so the signals that you send each other are clear. Listen to the Spirit of the Lord regarding communication: "Wherefore putting away lying, let every man speak truth to his neighbor; for we are members one of another" (Eph. 4:25).

If this is the kind of communication that the church should have, it should be even more so in marriage. This text simply says to be truthful in your communication. Honesty in communication keeps the signals clear between a husband and a wife. This includes passive lying. One practice and principle that Carole and I had to embrace was the principle of "if you say it, I believe you." This means if you're asked, "What's wrong?" and you respond dishonestly by saying, "Nothing," then don't be upset when I resume treating you as if nothing is wrong. Why? Because when asked, you said "Nothing." If you say it, I believe you. When we embraced this principle, "nothing" was replaced by "we can talk about it later" or "I had a problem with this or that." It trained us not to throw an opportunity for productive communication away by being dishonest. Even uncomfortable conversations make for good communication because of the clear signals they emit.

Good reception is simply the ability to listen well. Solomon says this about listening: "Spouting off before listening to the facts is both shameful and foolish" (Proverbs 18:13; NLT). Simply put, listen before you speak. James says, "Be swift to hear, slow to speak and slow to wrath" (James 1:19). Allowing yourself time to process and understand what your spouse is saying can save your marriage from a lot of misunderstanding.

Having a large coverage area simply gets at the scope of what you and your spouse can talk about. Healthy marital communication allows for the freedom to discuss and converse about ANYTHING, even though not necessarily EVERYTHING. This means no subject, topic, or matter is barred from conversation. The more intimate and personal the scope of your communication is, the closer and more trusting you become as a couple. However, for a conversation-friendly environment to be established, being judgmental and making assumptions must be shunned. You can't be judgmental and offensive and turn around and say, "Baby, you can talk to me about anything." This is a trap at best. Some of you reading this have experienced it first hand.

"Very few dropped calls" simply means that communication is followed through until resolution or understanding is established. There are so many issues that couples begin in conversation but end in one or both spouses' minds before full resolution. This is dangerous, because when only part of the story is understood and communicated, the other spouse is left to his or her own assumption and imagination to complete the story for him or herself. Don't drop something until you're ready to leave it alone. Now, I do understand that some issues require more than one conversation, but continue it until the end so that the "call of understanding" is not dropped.

Bad communication is generally dishonest. There are many faces of dishonesty. Some of those faces are:

- **Lying**. Downright untruth. Saying "I don't have ANY money at all," (while hiding a stash).
- **Omitting**. Purposely leaving something out. Saying, "I just went to the store, looked around, and came home" (not mentioning the $200 spent at the store).

- **Exaggerating**. Making something appear worse, bigger, better, or smaller than you know it to actually be. Saying, "I'm really, really worn out," when the real issue is you don't feel like cooking (wives) or filling the car with gas (husbands).

- **Extremism**. Using definite terminology for indefinite situations, such as, "You NEVER take me out anywhere"(wives, when you were just taken out last weekend), or "You ALWAYS leave me hanging in the bedroom" (husbands, when the reality is that you all have six kids together—how'd that happen?).

There are other faces of dishonesty we could explore, but I believe you get the point. Bad communication is built on dishonesty.

Non-existent communication... leaves you in as much suspense as the blank space in this sentence. Suspense gives rise to assumptions and unnecessary retaliation. Sometimes bad communication is easier to cope with than no communication.

Ugly communication is simply rude, nasty, offensive, and abusive communication that scars the heart, castrates the pride, disrupts the peace, stains the self-esteem, and cuts away at confidence.

Solomon says this in Proverbs 15:1: "A soft answer turneth away wrath but grevious words stir up anger." Ugly communication opens the curtains to the stage of deep animosity and secret resentment. Husbands and wives who use ugly communication will slowly turn their spouses into nothing more than roommates who are waiting for you to move out so that they can move in another tenant. Nothing suffocates the joy of marriage quite like ugly communication. It cuts off the air in the relationship until your spouse feels like he or she can't breathe in your presence and finds relief when you are not around.

We should pray that God gives us wisdom and self-control to exercise good communication so that we can grow together with our spouses, — and then grow old together.

Chapter 10

Restoring Communication

As established in the last chapter, one of the greatest challenges in marriage is communication—no matter how long you've been married. You and your spouse stood in front of the church, the judge, or the preacher. You repeated your vows one to another. You exchanged your rings and if you had a fancy wedding you lit the unity candles and were melodiously serenaded by a wedding singer. You were then pronounced man and wife and told to salute one another with a kiss. You then kissed the lips that would either be responsible for communicating the things that bring you up and down or for not communicating anything at all. Time passed by. You spend more time together. The rice and flowers fade into memory. The wedding has ended and now the marriage is in full swing. You used to be able to talk for hours on the phone prior to getting married. Now your communication is minimal, and if there is any communication at all, it only serves to drive you both further apart. Why does this happen? Why is communication one of the first things to fade in a marriage? What are some healthy and unhealthy ways to communicate? What are some differences between men and women in the area of communication? What are some ways to creatively resurrect dead communication in a marriage? I will attempt to discuss some of these things in this chapter in the ultimate hope that solutions can be explored and applied in the marriages of those whose happiness is obstructed by poor communication.

When the issue is not the "what" but the "how"

"Are you cooking dinner tonight?" he asks. "I took some meat down," she replies irritably. Or, "Why do you think I took some meat down?!" On the surface it may not seem like there was anything wrong with her response to his question. However, what you can't hear in these written words is that her voice is elevated and it is saturated with sarcasm. In and of itself there was nothing wrong with *what* she said, but it was *how* it was said that qualifies it as poor communication. Sarcasm, a form of mockery, is a passive-aggressive way of expressing anger. When a woman uses sarcasm with her husband it can be a very belittling experience for him. This is NOT okay. It is NOT a good practice to use sarcasm as a way to communicate. Neither is raising your voice in anger.

When a husband feels derided by his wife he may inwardly and secretly resent her for the way her communication makes him feel. Without knowing it, she burns the bridge of communication that she may soon have to cross. He may not say anything, but inwardly he may see her as a "hag with a nag." When this happens he may look for alternatives to conversing with her lest his questions be met with sarcasm and hostility. This kind of communication can happen for so long that it can begin to seem "normal." She may ask, "What was wrong with how I said that?" She will begin to lose her sense of reason and her objectivity. She may then fully embrace that way of communication, even to the point of assuming that the problem is with her husband's level of sensitivity and not her poor communication. When these "thinking disorders" solidify, it may become even harder for the situation to change.

The Bible has something to say about the "how" of communication that is just as applicable to marriage as it is in general. Solomon says, "A soft answer turneth away wrath, but grievous words stir up anger" (Prov. 15:1). Look at this same text in a simpler version: "A gentle answer deflects anger, but harsh words make tempers flare" (Prov. 15:1; NLT). Wives, practice saying things in ways that do not belittle or debase your husband. After all, he's your husband, not your son. "Well, if he starts acting like a man I will talk to him as a man," you may be thinking. Well, tell me, how much experience has the Lord given you in being a man? If you're not careful to change your manner of communication you may find that you become set in your ways. When this happens, the Scripture will be fulfilled: "It is better to dwell in a corner of the housetop, than with a brawling woman in a wide house" (Prov. 21:9). Let's look at the same text from a few simpler versions:

- "It's better to live alone in the corner of an attic than with a quarrelsome wife in a lovely home" (NLT).
- "It is better to live in a corner on the roof than inside the house with a quarreling wife" (NCV).
- "Better to live alone in a tumbledown shack than share a mansion with a nagging spouse" (The Message).

So, wives and soon to be wives, try not to communicate in a way that makes the housetop a good idea, or that turns the attic into a refuge, or a shack into a peaceful getaway.

No communication counts as bad communication

"I don't like to argue so I just won't say anything." This is the sentiment of many husbands who don't understand a woman's need to express herself. Often a husband's interpretation of his wife's expressiveness is that she's "nagging," "fussing," or "arguing" when in actuality it may simply be that she is expressing herself passionately. When a woman's expressiveness is misinterpreted in this way, to avoid what appears to be conflict brewing, her husband may emotionally "shut down." He may close his spirit and decide that it is better not to say anything. Though it seems like evading responsibility or emotionally running away, it's actually suppression. When this happens, all of the unexpressed feelings are pushed down and may ultimately build and accumulate within the husband until there is a breaking point. This is usually not a good situation. The truth is that not communicating at all is also bad communication. There is always a message being communicated—even in silence. The

Bible may not necessarily address in detail how a husband should communicate to his wife, but God does have a lot to say about communication in general, and what God says in general applies personally. The Bible talks about confrontation in Matthew 18:15–20, and these principles are applicable to our marriages. If your spouse "trespasses against you, go and tell." In other words, communicate and confront. Of course, this does not mean to dismiss the use of tact and discretion, but do communicate. I know what you may be saying: "But what if I communicate and he or she doesn't listen?" That's a good question. And to that I have a few replies:

- Understand that communication is not just sending signals but receiving signals. While it's important for her to listen, it is equally important for you to listen (as difficult as that may seem at times).

- Communicate with God as you are attempting to communicate with your spouse. Your communication with God can fan the flames of frustration if you begin to feel as if your efforts to communicate are not yielding any fruit. Frustration in a marriage can lead to the temptation to satisfy a temporary problem with a tragic solution. It's important that even if you struggle to stay grounded and spiritually connected at other times, you stay grounded and connected during frustration.

- Also, keep in mind that you can't MAKE your spouse respond to you the way you think he or she should. The Lord has given her a charge to submit to you and subject herself to your leadership (Eph. 5:21–25; 1 Pet. 3:1–7). If she decides to be rebellious and recalcitrant, she will have to answer to God. You can't force her to respond to you the way you want. You're her husband, not her father (plus at this point in her life her father couldn't force her either). Refocus. If the frustration is building and it seems unbearable and you've been suppressing your feelings in your attempts to communicate; if your communication hasn't been received in a way that is favorable to you, then refocus. That's right: refocus. You have more to think about, more to focus on, more to be consumed by than your present marital situation. After you've communicated with your spouse and God, get busy. Sitting idle thinking about the situation and wallowing in the frustration of the moment can give the adversary a foothold and allow him time to plant seeds of bitterness in your heart. Take a walk, wash the car, go to the gym, go to 7-Eleven and buy a Big Gulp, or finish a project. Do something until the storm of ill feelings passes.

In conclusion, it's never right to do wrong. You can't expect to be understood if you don't open up and communicate in your marriage. So, men and brethren, women and sisters, don't suppress, learn to express. You may find that this is what your spouse wanted all along.

Because you both said, "I do."

Chapter 11
The Challenge of Marriage

With all of the various ideas and truths about marriage that we can discuss, there is one marital truth that shines forth above all others: marriage is a beautifully harsh challenge. I know that this statement is paradoxical, but oftentimes so is marriage. No matter how easy some people make marriage appear, the reality is that great marriages do not just naturally happen; they are not automatic. Growth can often be a harsh process full of frustrations, temptations, irritations, and disappointments. Growing together will have you saying, "Thank you, Lord!" one day and "Help me, Lord!" the next. The person who can bring the biggest smile to your face can equally bring the biggest frown to your face.

Marriage can often be like a roller coaster,

complete with ups, downs, twists, turns, loops, jerks, turns, and drops. Then there are times when your mind takes you from the real to the ideal, and you start falling in love with what you wish your spouse would be like instead of who they actually are. In all honesty, Carole and I have divorced and remarried several time throughout our marriage. Now don't misunderstand me. We never went through filing the paperwork for a divorce, but in our moments of extreme, seemingly unbearable frustration, the idea of "I'm through with this" marched through our minds. Now, perhaps, this might be shocking to some of you. Well, if it is too shocking for you, think of the frustrations of your own marriage. If you're single and this is too shocking for you, then try getting married; watch the Lord graduate your understanding. The reality is, a great marriage is not one that doesn't have its challenges, but rather one that survives its challenges and the couple draws closer because of them. You'll never know the true quality of an untested marriage.

I've learned that the Lord doesn't always fix a tense, broken marriage by means of a good counselor. Now, being a counselor myself, I do not discredit or minimize the effectiveness of marriage counseling, but I will say that counseling is not a cure-all or fix-all for troubled marriages. You see, counseling is human intervention and is sometimes needed to get to a place of resolve, but I've found that heavenly intervention is more effective. However, please know that the Lord's intervention is not always convenient. Sometimes His intervention is very uncomfortable. When a couple becomes consumed with the tension in their marriage, sometimes the Lord intervenes by refocusing the couple onto things that matter. It's so easy to get hung up on things that really don't matter even in marriage. All of the petty issues that obstruct marital happiness and progress can be eclipsed by things that are more important. The Lord will sometimes use "together problems" to fix marital tension. The Lord has the awesome ability to heal something by means of sickness. What a strange paradox! God can use SICKNESS to HEAL? He can use PAIN to bring RELIEF? Absolutely! Look at some of these scenarios:

- A couple having a hard time getting along is being forced to pull together because someone near and dear to the both of them gets gravely ill.

- A couple struggling to get over some offenses from the past have to refocus because one of them becomes sick and disabled.

- A couple starts growing apart and stops

spending time with each other: sleeping in different rooms, driving in separate vehicles, having separate social lives. That is, until one of them is laid off and has to get rid of a car or downsize their home and they no longer have time for separate social lives.

- A couple loses focus on what's important and gets hung up and consumed with their marital tension until something happens to one of their children, which demands that they get over the marital spats that were driving a wedge between them.

I believe you get the point. Though it's very uncomfortable when bad circumstances fall on any couple, sometimes God will use these trials to refocus a marriage onto things that demand togetherness. He will use something uncomfortable to save a marriage from something fatal to its existence. This is a harsh way for a broken marriage to be fixed, but sometimes it becomes necessary so that a couple will stop being so selfish and thinking only about themselves. If we pray and seek God's help with a sincere heart the Lord will answer our prayers, but understand that His answer is not always what we anticipate. Sometimes He has to break something to fix something.

There are several circumstances and situations that will bring clarity to the things in life that really matter. So what if he snores when he sleeps! So what if she raised her voice at you! So what if he doesn't put the toilet seat down! So what if she hasn't cooked in a while! So what if he didn't tell you he wrote that check! So what if she didn't get a chance to clean up the kitchen! All of these issues pale in comparison to other matters that have to do with life and loved ones. Don't let the Lord have to use brokenness to fix your marriage. However, if He does, you may find that your marriage works better in broken circumstances. After all, you asked the Lord for a little help because, remember: you're married!

PART 2

Lord, I Need a Little Help Here, Please... I'm Single!

Chapter 12

What's Wrong with Being Single?

I f you live in the South (or even if you don't), then this is all too familiar to you: You go visit some family or friends you have not seen in quite some time. They're excited to see you. They greet you with great hugs of excitement and joy. "It's so good to see you," they say. You return the compliment. They begin to question you about how you are doing. You brace yourself because you know that the infamous, irritating question is going to find its way into the conversation. You know, that question that has you feeling like something is wrong with you; that question that fills you with frustration and leaves you feeling inadequate at times. I am referring to the question that seems inescapable when confronted by family, friends, and longtime acquaintances who have not seen you for a while. You guessed it: the big

"Are you married yet?" question. Perhaps out of your frustration and irritation you entertain thoughts of sarcastic ways to reply to this annoying question. Some of those replies may sound like this: "Oh, I didn't know it was state law for me to be married by now," or "Do you see a ring on my finger yet?" or "Why do you ask, were you going to propose?" or "No, I forgot, but I'll do it tomorrow." Many of these sarcastic replies are products of the irritability that comes with being asked if you're married. This leads to the feeling of being pressured into marriage for the sake of being able to say, "I'm finally married."

It seems as if being single is a curse. Some may even see it as a taboo. However, I propose to you this question: What's wrong with being single? In this chapter I want to deal with some of the issues faced by unmarried people in the Lord's church everywhere. Know that just because you're not married it does not mean that there is something wrong with you, neither is it an indication of abnormality. Quite frankly, there are certain freedoms that single people can enjoy that would be unacceptable in marriage. For instance, if at 2:00 A.M. you want to go to a Waffle House for some grits, bacon, and eggs, without thinking twice and without explanation, you can go satisfy that early morning craving. Should you ever want to save your money and take a trip to Hawaii simply because you've never been there before, you can get the ticket, board the plane and be basking in the sun on a beach in Honolulu sipping on a strawberry smoothie. Not only that, but the scope of who you minister to and the time you have to minister is much broader than it would be if you were married.

I often used to wonder why people would move here from places like Hawaii, the Philippines, Jamaica, or another beautiful tropical island; it seems that most people dream about living on a tropical fantasy island. They're trying to get here and we're trying to get there—how ironic is that? Perhaps it's because the main thing that is advertised about the tropics are the beaches and resorts, never the poverty-stricken neighborhoods or the poor economy. The same is true for the United States: the opportunity to make money and the better economy are highlighted, but never the high taxes, violence, and bad politics.

In a similar way, in my twenty plus years of ministering to the people of God, I've found that while there are many single people who desire to cross the fence line into marriage, there are almost as many people who want to cross back over the fence line and be single again. I'm not suggesting that this is right, but I am suggesting that things aren't always what they seem. While there are many things you gain when you cross the threshold of matrimony, there are also many things that you lose. Married or single, no position gives you all of the benefits of both. It can actually be hazardous to a marriage if people don't first enjoy being single. It's too late to enjoy being single when you're married. Again, marriage is beautiful and honorable, but so is the freedom that comes with being single.

Marriage is not a Commandment

Who says that you must marry by a certain point in your life? Who says that marriage is a requirement to make it to Heaven's door? The Bible does say this about marriage in Hebrews 13:4: "Marriage is honorable in all, and the bed undefiled: but whore-mongers and adulterers God will judge." The word that is used for honorable is *timios*, which means to be held as of great price, precious, or valuable. The Bible again declares in 1 Corinthians 6:9: "But if they cannot contain let them marry; for it is better to marry than to burn." While there are great benefits to being married, it is also important to understand that God does not command everyone to be married. It may very well be in the plan of God for some individuals to remain single; it may be meant for those individuals to be "eunuchs for the kingdom's sake" (Matt. 19:11, 12). Is it God's will that everyone marry? The inspired apostle Paul says something very interesting in 1 Corinthians 7:7: "For I would that all men were even as I myself. But every man hath his proper gift of God, one after this manner, and another after that." What is Paul referring to when he says "even as I myself"? No doubt he was referring to his status as an unmarried person. Please do not misunderstand. Marriage is a beautiful thing, especially when it's beautiful (hope you got that). However, unmarried people should not feel abnormal, irregular, or atypical simply because they do not have a spouse. God called it honorable and blessed, but He never declares in His Word that marriage is an absolute must. Sometimes it's easy to succumb to the pressure of watching other people booed—to the point where you might slip into a momentary covetousness. It's very common, especially in church settings.

Then there is the issue of libido. Sexual tension is a legitimate issue. We might as well be honest about it. Sometimes there is a lack of sensitivity on the part of married people; sometimes they oversimplify abstinence. It seems easy to do when husbands lay next to curves, hips, lips, and thighs every night. It seems easy also when wives end their day cuddled up under biceps, pecs, and triceps. Some argue, "Marriage IS a commandment if you want to avoid fornication." To this I say, absolutely! But beware that you don't marry sex; you marry a spouse. The excitement of sex fades, and if you're not content with what you are left with when sex becomes old, then your latter end may be worse than the first. Unfortunately, there may be some reading this book who already know how timeworn sex can become—even though you've never married. There are commandments in marriage that are inclusive, such as being loving, caring, sacrificing for your spouse; and obeying, submitting to, and giving yourself to your spouse. If you're not ready to keep these commandments, then you may not be ready to keep the commandment of marrying to avoid fornication. God knows your frustrations. However, your focus can either extinguish your frustration or intensify it. Perhaps a change of focus may be therapeutic so you can avoid becoming consumed with what you feel you're missing out on by remaining single. You're commanded and instructed to be faithful to God—not necessarily to be married.

Chapter 13

Desperation: Compromises and Complications

With all of the pressure that is often placed on the unmarried to find someone, settle down, and get married, there is a temptation that grows out of impatience called desperation. Desperation is a very powerful feeling. Unhealthy desperation creates unhealthy ambition that can easily lead to unethical and ultimately sinful patterns of living. Desperation can come from a strong desire for companionship, or it can come from a strong desire for intimacy. Sometimes the desire for some kind of intimacy can be so strong that you'd even settle for artificial intimacy just to get through the moment. What is artificial intimacy, you ask? Well, it's the kind of intimacy that Judah fell into in Genesis 38:15–16. Judah, while in mourning over the loss of his wife, saw a woman sitting at the entrance of a town he traveled to and simply wanted to have sexual relations with her. No emotional ties, no strings attached, no commitment. He just wanted passion divorced from intimacy, which made it artificial intimacy. Look at the text in the New Living Translation:

> Judah noticed her and thought she was a prostitute, since she had covered her face.
>
> So he stopped and propositioned her. "Let me have sex with you," he said, not realizing that she was his own daughter-in-law. (Gen. 38: 15–16)

All he wanted was a moment of intimacy without commitment: artificial intimacy. He wanted the pleasurable feelings that come with intimacy, without the commitment that comes with intimacy. Unbeknownst to Judah, the woman was his deceased son's widow. Sometimes desperation can come from depressing circumstances, the frustration of loneliness, the envy of others around you and their companions. Whatever the case, desperation can blind you to wisdom.

Desperation may cause an individual to settle for mediocrity. Desperation can grow out of being comparative in your thinking. However, desperation mostly comes from feelings of deprivation, feeling as if you are being deprived of something that you really need or even want. This was one of the ways that Satan deceived Eve in Genesis 3. He ignited within her feelings of being deprived of something she needed, in this case the forbidden fruit. As soon as he created the desperation in her, (the apple looked good for food and pleasing to the eye), she became blind to everything she had access to. She just had to have fruit from THAT tree. She compromised her freedom, her relationship with God, her home, and her paradise. In her desperation, she compromised everything that was perfect, pure, and sufficient for her and her husband, and of course, he did the same. She settled for a limited amount of forbidden fruit in exchange for a vast garden of unrestricted, unlimited fruit. In other words, out of desperation she lowered her God-given standards and gave up freedom for bondage, happiness for sorrow.

If you are an unmarried person, it is important for you to understand that God sets the standards. He knows your needs before you need them, and He knows your desires when they are but passing thoughts. Jesus said it this way in Matthew 6:8: "For your father knoweth what things ye have need of, before ye ask him." Don't become so desperate for companionship, affection, or even intimacy that you will settle for less than what God would have for you. Your desperation can lead to unwise decisions, which will leave you regretful and resentful toward the object of your desperation. The ironic thing is that oftentimes when we jump into relationships out of desperation, not long after, what we were looking for prances or trots by—but we're stuck with our decision. I can't recall the countless number of brothers and sisters who have given the testimony that as soon as they settled for a mediocre relationship all of the "could have beens" appeared. Be patient. Know that God loves you and longs to be first in your life. Wait on Him. If you really needed what you so desperately want, then He would have given it to you by now. Trust His way, His will, His Word, and His timing.

How do you make up for this strong desire for companionship? Build upon the relationships that are already active in your life. Work on being a better sister, brother, cousin, friend, parent, son, or daughter. If you fall for the trap of desperation you may very well still make it to the Canaan of your goals and to your aspirations of happiness and contentment, but it may take you forty years instead of eleven days if you waste your time chasing and settling out of desperation. "Meantime" compromises can lead to "long time" complications.

Chapter 14

A Strong Woman or the Wrong Woman?

It's interesting to hear how people, particularly women, define what it means to be a strong woman. The diversity of opinions as to what this means is about as vast as the distance from the east to the west. Generally speaking, their definition of strength is defined by several factors including personal experience, secondhand experience, fears, apprehensions, family of origin, cultural influence, and religious influence, just to name a few. Yet at the end of the day, there remains a fine line between strength and other character traits that are often mistaken for strength. Some character traits that are often mistaken for strength are pride, stubbornness, fear, anger, aggression, manipulation, inflexibility, and sabotage (again, just to name a few). Bearing these characteristics does not necessarily make you a "strong" woman but can actually make you the "wrong woman." There is a difference, and God has something to say about what a strong woman is and what she is not. Explore with me.

I can't tell you how many times I've seen women's conferences and ladies' day program ads come across my desk with the theme "Who can find a virtuous woman?" or "Being a 'Proverbs 31 woman,'" or something of the like. As a matter of fact, nowadays there seems to be more conferences and symposiums for women than there are for men. (Brothers, we've got to do better.) A lot of time, energy, and finances are invested in empowering women to be the kind of women who please God. This is definitely a good endeavor, but as with any attempt to empower anyone, the first thing that must be established is who is being empowered and what are they being empowered to do? You empower a good person and he becomes good and useful. You empower a corrupt person and he becomes worse and even more destructive. Quality of character should be improved before a person is empowered. That's why the new birth comes before the empowerment of the Spirit of God. A bitter person empowered in that bitterness becomes increasingly destructive. It is important to have a thorough, honest, and realistic understanding of self. If you don't understand yourself then why would you expect someone else to? Know your character. Are you short tempered? Impatient? Moody? Selfish? Self-centered? Manipulative? These are things that may be more painful to admit than you would think. Some of these character traits do better without the compounding complication of a relationship.

Your past has a lot to do with what you perceive as strength or weakness. For instance, if you have a history of emotional abuse, being hurt, disappointed, cheated on, let down, or abandoned, then you may see being a strong woman as being a very guarded, closed, serious, and distrusting woman. However, this is not strength. It's actually fear. You can become the product of what you fear so you put on armor to ensure that it doesn't happen again. It's a self-protective mechanism that feels like strength but is actually loneliness. Somehow subconsciously you feel better being incarcerated by your own insecurities than being free to feel again. Safety is your number-one policy. Positive clichés are used to veil this fear: "I can do bad all by myself." "I don't need nobody in my life but God." "I refuse to be hurt again." Please don't misunderstand me. There is nothing wrong with wanting to avoid being hurt, let down or abused, but if you have become emotionally numb, then while you may be safe from feeling pain, you're also guarded from feeling pleasure.

I can recall going to the dentist and having

extensive dental work done including an extraction and a deep gum cleaning. To move forward with the procedure they had to anesthetize me really well. This was good because Lord knows I didn't want to feel the pain of all of that drilling and pulling. However, when all of the oral trauma was over, the numbness continued. So when I arrived home and my daughters greeted me with a kiss I couldn't feel it. Shucks! I wished I could just turn off the numbness at will, but it didn't work like that. When it was time to eat, ugh! You guessed it. I wasn't able to taste my food or know whether or not I was biting my lip. Why? Because the same pain-killing numbness that blocked the pain of my dental work also blocked the pleasure of a meal or a kiss of greeting from my babies.

The same is true when we use emotional anesthesia to protect ourselves from the vulnerability of trusting friendships or relationships. It's often harder to turn off such numbness than it is to turn it on. You may miss a lot of potentially great things in the process of becoming vulnerable and trusting again. There are absolutely no guarantees that people are not going to let you down from time to time—just like there are no guarantees that every day will be a sunny day. But you don't superglue an umbrella to your skin, do you? Again, being guarded and callous, closed and hard-up doesn't make you a strong woman; it makes you the wrong woman.

Some believe that being independent makes you a strong woman. I would have to agree that it does take strength to be independent, but it takes even more strength to know how to turn that off and be passive enough to lean on somebody from time to time. "I make my own money," "I pay my own car note and have keys to my own place," and on and on that conversation goes. Again, those things do take strength to do. But it also takes great strength, humility, and meekness to be able to do those things yet still subject yourself to someone who wants to do that for you. God created the universe and had Heaven at His command—that's strength. But an even greater display of strength was when He contorted and shrank enough to be cooped up in a human womb and then was born in a stable and breastfed and coddled and cradled. That's even greater strength.

A strong woman knows how to turn off the pride of independence and be passive long enough to be served and catered to without having to spend all of her time trying to prove the point that she can do it herself. Yes, you can clearly open doors for yourself, but can you be womanly enough to let a man open a door for you? You can buy your own dinner—you've proven that—but can you put that aside long enough to be treated to a nice dinner without feeling you need to make it clear that you could have just as easily paid the bill yourself? Now, I'm not suggesting that you become passive to the point of taking abuse, but what I am asking is this: Can you be strong enough to go without your emotional anesthesia for a moment or two? It makes sense that it's hard to find a husband when you've spent all your life training yourself not to need one. Now, this is just one perspective.

As you read this, you don't necessarily have to agree with this because there are some women who define this as "strength." But I'm suggesting that although it may very well be protective, it isn't necessarily strength. A lot of women are so guarded because they have taken abuse from men over the years. This I do understand. However, the challenge is to avoid becoming the very thing you despise. There is nothing at all wrong with being cautious, but fear is a love blocker. There are some of you reading this who do well with platonic or love relationships until there is an attempt to go a little deeper or get a little more serious in the relationship; then you sabotage it so that no one can get close enough to you to hurt you. Bear in mind that if a relationship is not close enough to hurt it is also not close enough to help.

Strong woman or wrong woman? The Bible says in 1 Peter 3:2-5 that there is something powerful about a wife (or even a woman for that matter) who places more emphasis in beautifying her character before her appearance. A meek and gentle spirit. These are fading qualities today as more and more women seek independence. There is nothing wrong with a woman having independence, if she knows how to regulate her spirit.

I'd be remiss if I didn't talk about the other extreme. Silence doesn't always indicate strength either. Some people are passive to a fault. There are certain situations that call for more than a passive "Whatever you say, hon." It is dangerous to be passive at a time that demands aggression and assertiveness. Just as Jesus understood what He was supposed to tolerate, so should a woman. This is not only in her relationship with a man but in every relationship she's engaged in. Strength is not the ability to control external success but the ability to control internal character. There are plenty of sour successful women who have attitudes that serve as friend repellents, boyfriend repellents, and companion repellents.

I trust that you understand that a strong woman is one who is virtuous and knows how to have a sports car but still drive the speed limit. Other qualities might look like they make you strong, but as character is revealed over time it becomes clear that it's not STRONG: it's just wrong.

Chapter 15

Examining Men

Just as it is important for women to examine themselves under a microscope to differentiate between a "strong woman" and a "wrong woman"; so must single men. The simple reality is, whatever trait you have as an individual you carry into your relationships. An angry man will carry that anger into his relationships no matter what they are. And though characteristics can be suppressed for a season they will soon burst forth given the right set of circumstances. Suffice it to say, a man should know what's gotten into him before he can understand what he's getting into when it comes to relationships. Whatever is in you as a man gets into the relationship and will ultimately affect the relationship positively or negatively. Just as women can mistake stubbornness for strength, men can mistake being gaudy for being goodly, or goodly for being Godly. The reality is, they are not synonymous.

I want to begin by defining certain terms I will use in this chapter. First, let's look at what the word gaudy means and at what is a gaudy man. Well, gaudy is defined as excessively showy or cheaply showy in a tasteless way. A gaudy man is the man who is on a constant expedition for attention and will go overboard to acquire this attention. Gaudy men will step on anyone, put down anyone, and embarrass anyone to get attention. There is absolutely nothing inherently wrong with wanting attention. As a matter of fact, this is something that we have desired since our days as children. I'm sure anyone reading this can recount all the times that we did something and uttered the words, "Mommy, look at me," or "Daddy, look at me." This was our effort to get the attention of someone we wanted to impress. At some point as boys we should have grown out of that as we entered manhood. However, it is unfortunate to note that instead of growing out of it some of us men have grown even deeper into it. We're no longer saying "Mommy, look at me!" or "Daddy, look at me!"; but now we're nonverbally saying, "Everybody look at me." Gaudy men have a tendency to sacrifice almost anything in exchange for attention, especially from women.

It's amazing to observe the atmospheric impact

that a very attractive woman has when she walks into a fitness center filled with testosterone-rich, protein-shake-drinking, tight-t-shirt-wearing men. It's almost as if the presence of the attractive female specimen has the same effect on men as an energy drink. Then begins the unspoken signals of, "Hey, look at me!" Some men will go so far in their gaudiness as to place an unreasonable amount of weight on their bench-press bar to impress a woman who may not even be paying them any mind. Or what about the man who becomes the life of the party so that he can be the center of attention for a woman he feels is attractive. He starts insulting other people and overexerting himself trying to be funny so as to impress and stand out to some attractive female. Again, truthfully speaking, desiring a little attention is not a problem, except that sometimes gaudiness can be deceptive. It can be a temporary display of something that is not a consistent reality. A gaudiness-driven man will be charming as long as it takes to win the trophy of attention that he so desires. A gaudy man puts his best foot forward while secretly hiding his stanky leg.

However, a man of confidence will not compromise or overexert himself simply because he is who he is, he has what he has, and he does what he does. Take it or leave it. Gaudiness can also come across at times as desperation, which can often be an immediate turn off. It takes an honest man to notice this and get his gaudiness under control. Sampson went through a period of gaudiness in an attempt to impress Delilah, which ultimately caused him to end up blind, bald, and bound. Personally, I've learned that it doesn't take long for attention to dissolve after it is acquired and the effort it takes to get it may not even be worth it. Nothing is wrong with wanting to be noticed catching a fish, but if you go overboard, not only will you miss the catch, you'll become shark bait. The gaudy man has game but doesn't play fair.

Now what I mean when I use the word "goodly" or when I use the phrase "goodly man" is simply a man who is fine in appearance. As men we sometimes have the same passion with keeping our outward appearance attractive as women do. No man invests time in trying to be unattractive. Even if there are some things about our appearance that we don't like we still attempt to compensate for those things through other means. If our weight is a problem, we step up our gear game. If we have physical challenges, we compensate with our masculine "swag." Contrary to popular belief, men are just as concerned with their goodly disposition as many women are. However, appearance and character are not always congruent. It doesn't matter how groomed a skunk is; at the end of the day it still stinks. Physique is not a substitute for character. Unfortunately, because appearance is an important thing today for women, there are some men who dump all of their efforts on their "goodliness" while leaving their character completely ungroomed and uncouth. There is some biblical legitimacy to the "goodly" man. Observe the following texts:

- "So Potiphar gave Joseph complete administrative responsibility over everything he owned. With Joseph there, he didn't worry about a thing—except what kind of food to eat! Joseph was a very handsome and well-built young man, and Potiphar's wife soon began to look at him lustfully. 'Come and sleep with me,' she demanded" (Gen. 39:6–7; NLT).

- "His son Saul was the most handsome man in Israel—head and shoulders taller than anyone else in the land" (I Sam. 9:2; NLT).

- "Then Samuel asked, 'Are these all the sons you have?' 'There is still the youngest,' Jesse replied. 'But he's out in the fields watching the sheep and goats.' 'Send for him at once,' Samuel said. 'We will not sit down to eat until he arrives.' So Jesse sent for him. He was dark and handsome, with beautiful eyes. And the LORD said, 'This is the one; anoint him'" (1 Sam. 16:11–12; NLT).

Of course, the list goes on and on: Absalom, Sampson, and others. So again, there is some biblical legitimacy to handsome or "goodly" men. However, it is important to understand that the gift-wrapping is not always an accurate prediction of the value of the gift. God has called us to do more than just look good, brethren.

Finally, there's the godly man, meaning the DEVOUT man or the man who is devoted to a pursuit, belief, or mode of God-like behavior. A godly man is permeated by the influence of God. You don't have to wonder or second-guess a man when his life is heavily influenced by the person and purpose of God in his life. Now, please don't misunderstand me. Godly does not mean that you have to walk around quoting Scriptures every day or be so sterile that people are afraid to relax around you. This is a superficial kind of pious veneer that doesn't attract people to want to know God, but actually repels people from you. This is what Paul calls a "form of godliness" in 2 Timothy 3:5. When a man is like this he actually makes being godly unattractive and burdensome.

So what is a godly man? What kinds of things does a godly man do? How does a godly man behave? Being godly is not complicated. I want to take a very biblical and definitional approach to this, and then a practical approach. Godliness in Scripture comes from a word that means to be pious or religious. Yet on a practical everyday level, godly describes the kind of person who has both an awareness of God and a respect for God. Hmm: awareness and respect.

I can remember when I was in junior high, whenever our main teacher was going to be absent they would send in a substitute teacher. I know now that it couldn't have been any fun being a substitute teacher. Well, anyway, when the sub would come into the classroom many times the students would continue their private conversations and whatever mischief they were into. We had an awareness of the sub's presence, but because there was no respect for the sub, his presence didn't affect our behavior. However, the next day when our regular teacher came into the room a silence came over the class, not only because of her presence, but also because of the respect or reverence we had for her. A godly man keeps both an awareness of and a respect for the presence of God in his life. There are boundaries that such a man will not cross because of his awareness and respect for God. To have only an awareness of God is only a "form of godliness" as was mentioned earlier in this chapter.

So how does that fit into the context of this chapter? The godly man maintains a respect for God no matter what he's involved in or where he is or who he is around. It becomes amazingly apparent that he knows that God is present, and thus, he shows his respect for God by how he interacts with others. Again, it doesn't mean that he's sterile and arrogant, but it is similar to how a child acts when his parent is in the room versus how a child acts when he's away from his parent. So, a girlfriend is not the primary motivation for the godly man; neither is money or looks. God is the godly man's motivation. Everything else is a secondary motivation.

Now that we have defined the terms and explained the characteristics of the terms, the question that remains is: Are you a gaudy man, a goodly man, or a godly man? Someone may ask, "Is it possible to be all three?" To this I answer, yes it is, but not in equal proportions. One will stand out above the other two. You'll either be a gaudy man who is preoccupied with his goodly look and tries to appear godly. Or you'll be a goodly man who uses his looks to be gaudy and creates the image of being godly. Or you'll be a godly man who is gaudy for God and looks goodly primarily to God first and men second.

Chapter 16

Getting Married vs. Being Married

Marriage is one of the hottest topics today on the Internet, in social networks and churches, and even on the silver screen. While I have to admit that it appears that statistically women are more preoccupied with marriage than men are, the subject of marriage is still valued by men nonetheless. May the Lord help us when marriage loses its global appeal. In every generation, several artists in the music industry release songs that are centered on the concept of marriage. Just about every year around what some recognize as "marriage season" (between May and July), movies hit the big screen that have marriage and family as their central themes. Marriages, or the violation of its sanctity, is often at the center of the "juiciest" controversial issues in today's society. In

Christianity, marriage is very much emphasized (as it should be).

Somewhere in the back of many a single person's mind is the idea of meeting someone, falling in love with them, laughing with them, taking walks in the park while holding hands, coming up with pet names for each other, and wining and dining each other until finally he gets down on one knee at dinner or at some other public venue and pops the big question: "I want to be with you for the rest of my life; will you marry me?" With tears welling up in her eyes, she looks at him and looks at the ring, then looks at him again, and finally with a trembling voice she says, "Yes, I will marry you" (while everyone around them begins applauding). Then our mind jumps to the altar: big church, beautiful floral arrangements, bridesmaids, groomsmen, ring bearer, flower girl, arched floral arrangement, preacher, vows, "I do's," romantic Hollywood kiss, pictures, and reception with your traditional electric slide. Unfortunately, just as the credits scroll up at that point in a Tyler Perry production, so do they in many people's minds. The scene is one of GETTING married...not BEING married.

If we took inventory of the world around us we might discover that there are more people who want to get married than who want to be married. There are many people who have the wedding more in mind than they do the marriage. Many of you reading this who are married should be able to attest that it's not just that simple, unless of course you're starring in some kind of blockbuster production. Otherwise, the fact remains that BEING married has greater and deeper challenges than GETTING married. The same is true with the Christian life. It's easier to BECOME a Christian than to BE one. There are a lot of people who have gotten this mixed up and have become more intrigued with the IDEA of marriage than with BEING married in a practical sense.

I'd like to discuss a few distinct differences between GETTING married and BEING married as we explore this ever so relevant topic. First, getting married means that you repeat vows. BEING married means you keep them. The vows at a wedding ceremony can sound so romantic and euphoric, especially when read with passion. However, I wonder, do people really take the time to hear what they are saying? Do we hear the promises we're making? "With ALL my earthly possessions," "forsaking ALL others," "love, cherish AND OBEY"? These are some monumental promises. There are no "but if" clauses in these vows (unless of course you take the prenuptial route). Now, while I have to be honest and say that the vows themselves are not in the Scriptures per say, God does have a lot to say about keeping vows. Let's read what the Lord has to say about making and keeping a vow:

> Don't make rash promises, and don't
> be hasty in bringing matters before
> God.

> After all, God is in heaven, and you are
> here on earth. So let your words be few.
> (Ecc. 5:2; NLT)

Wow! God says that we should not make rash promises, meaning thoughtless, hasty, and idle promises. God has an expectation when we make a vow. As a matter of fact, it's only logical that expectation should follow a vow. Expectation creates dependency. When we expect things, we depend on those things to happen or take place. Thus, keeping a vow is essential to the expectation and the dependency of the one we made it to. GETTING married entails the RECITATION of the vows, while BEING married entails the DEMONSTRATION of the vows. GETTING married involves the EXPRESSION of the vows, while BEING married involves the EXPERIENCE of the vows. Now, do you want to BE married or just GET married?

Next, getting married is public with occasional private moments. Being married is private with occasional public moments. There are several things that are easier to do in front of the gazing eyes of the public. Weddings can be very public. The audience consists of friends, family, and the mysterious group of unknown who show up at just about every public wedding. Everyone watches. The women in the audience look at the bride's outfit from the top of the veil to the end of the long flowing train. The men in the audience look at the bridesmaids (just kidding, I think). However, everyone is looking, listening, and taking everything in that they can see and hear. Of course, there are some looks that are private between the groom and bride that the audience is not privy to. That's GETTING married.

Then comes BEING married. The audience leaves after devouring the buffalo wings, meatballs, carrot and celery sticks, and cake and drinking the bubbly. BEING married begins; this is a very private, undisclosed state of being. If the romance and love was a GETTING married type of love and romance, it will fade in the privacy of BEING married. Heaven's truth about marriage is that there is no other earthly relationship described by God as two becoming one. Read what God says:

> This explains why a man leaves his
> father and mother and is joined to his
> wife, and the two are united into one.
> (Gen. 2:24; NLT)

Hmm! This is the only earthly relationship that

the Bible says has this characteristic. Not even between a parent and child is this kind of closeness described. This is a private connection, an exclusive closeness, an inseparable tie, an RSVP of one individual to another. This is what must be maintained in BEING married. GETTING married is the public face of what should be a private exclusive relationship. Now, do you want to BE married or just GET married?

Made in the USA
San Bernardino, CA
06 May 2016